D4

495

IRIDIUM

LIVRES
DC
BOOKS

Cover design by Gerald Luxton.

Designed and typeset in Palatino by DCAD Enterprises, Montreal.

Printed and bound in Canada by Hignell.

Dépot légal, Bibliothèque nationale du Québec
and the National Library of Canada, 4th trimester, 1993.

Versions of these poems have appeared in the following periodicals
and anthologies: *Canadian Literature, Matrix, The Moosehead Review,
Late Romantics,* by R. Allen, S. Luxton, and M. Teicher, *The Lyric
Paragraph,* ed. R. Allen, *The Moosehead Anthology,* various editors, etc.

The publishers acknowledge the assistance of The Canada Council.

Canadian Cataloguing in Publication Data.

Luxton, Steve, 1946--
Iridium

Poems.
ISBN 0-919688-40-3 (bound) —
ISBN 0-919688-42-X (pbk.)

1. Title.

PS8573.U98174 1993   C811'.54   C93-090608-X
PR9199.3.L89174   1993

DC Books, 1495 rue de l'Eglise, Box 662, Montreal, Que., H4L 4V9

IRIDIUM

STEVE LUXTON

For Susan Palmer

*Thanks also for help and advice and inspiration to Robert
Allen, Louis Dudek, Bill Furey, Ralph Gustafson, Keith
Henderson, John Ruttner, Anne Stone, Aylene Sullivan,
and many others.*

Contents

11. Hermit Crab's Song
12. Iridium
14. Bedouin Song
16. Devon Church-Goers
18. Fragment
19. Sea Change
20. Among Young Bohemians
22. Yucatan
24. Meniscus: An Essay on Water Striders
26. Rest-Stop at a Lake Superior Mill-Town
27. Babyface
28. Citycountry
30. Muse on de Bullion Street
32. Monstrous Restoration Fantasy:
    Storm over Montreal
35. Moment at a Garden Party
36. Knights at the Chemical Dump
38. The Escape Attempt: An Anti-Semiotic Song
40. Country Dark
41. At the River's Side
42. Evening Walk by Lake Superior
45. Old Fisherman
46. After the Flu: Spring
47. Woman Bathing in the Rouge River
48. Reflections on the Lake Superior Shoreline
50. Winter Lovers
51. The Old Indians

Contents (cont'd)

52. Drinking Beer on a Sand-Hill
    in Northwestern Nebraska
54. Going through the Poetry Files
55. West Coast Pier
56. My Antique Coin Collection
57. Surprises
58. Departures
60. Retro-Man
61. Ode to a Country Stone Pile
62. [Untitled]
64. Ascent
65. Rimer's Lament
66. Psycho-Gothic
67. Morning After: At the Dacha
68. Doll's House
70. Poetry
71. Autumn Dress Code
72. Gothic Piscatorial
74. Four A.M. Piece

IRIDIUM

Hermit Crab's Song

I live in
whatever
turns up.

Like a small dawn landscape
a pink quilt washes up.

I curl on it,
stay awhile.

I do this now.
I have no fear of this.

Here's an old culvert
clear at both ends.
No flood backs up.
Fine: a room with two views.

Anything
that turns up
I inhabit
in blessed vagrancy.

Things people throw away,
their broken beds,
homes, dreams,
mean for me
a lucky day....

Things that turn up
I live in.

Iridium

These days sleep is
        deepest
    — a sea-abyss
      before waking,
though I know nothing of it directly.

What I know are
        dreams,
vast and weirdly coiled,
    medieval chart-edge monsters
that, thrashing, endlessly
            ascend,
while I cling like a limpet
        or dazed Ahab.

Mon ami,
    the things far down that dark
I have sensed but not seen!
    — maybe just glimpsed,
brushing outlandish phosphorescence
    on me.

Once,
    (unbidden flashback!)
I befriended a drunk, born
        in the forbidden Gobi.
Before memory,
    he was spirited out
of that marvellous waste
        of vanished monster eggs.

"If only I could get back there now!"
he'd lament.

In the profoundest pit of the sea
eggs heap,
fated never to hatch.
They have contracted to stone.
From among them,
worried by surface currents,
forever strayed,
dream-things bulge upwards
like prehistoric breath....

Otherworldly,
saurian, foetal,
their eyes perfect offsets of others
— ancient, glassy,
seized in some forgotten catastrophe,
never to be used,
somehow they rise in my head,
blink open:

Their pupils distill a scene
of lost, entangled
bottom
which I, floating on
my usual waking surface,
must drown thoroughly
to see....

Bedouin Song

Some autumn nights I dreamed I was a Bedouin,
    heart-broken,
        drifting the city's Main.
My nightmare camel was dubbed Byron,
        a beast with lumps
    the world had recently added to.

I modelled all the gifts you left me:
    floor-length smock,
        Turkish slippers,
a liberation button on a Palestinian head-dress askew....
    I even had a weapon
                — the Italian garlic press.

Mine was a strange way to carry on,
        even for a dream.
A nomad now, I whiled away the days in a greasy spoon
    snuffling tears,
        bizarrely apparelled.
Playing Lawrence of Ammonia,
I scribbled lunatic ghazals about us:
        how we must get back together!

Oh I traipsed those dunes of misery,
        the city's streets,
mixing with bums, outpatients
    and dealers of powder
(the latter scorned me, despised my licit pains,
but the monkeys-on-their-backs adored Byron.)

Nights,
    with my heavy effects,
I roosted on the catwalk of the monstrous
      high billboard
 at Mount Royal and St. Urbain,
   under a soft-core poster from Club Med.

She, the houri of the ad,
     was thirty,
lavish feet of sand-golden flesh
  and looked a lot like you,
      far away eyes
beaming across the landscape
  free,
     now that you are unencumbered of me.

Yes,
   a strange way to live it was
       and sleep.
The visions of loss were unforgettable.
I awoke once
     into a drugstore-yellow dawn,
       — battered by winds.
Across the billboard above
  my night-tears glittered and swarmed,
   like rain up a windshield,
      rising.
Byron, my fever-eyed camel,
     flywalked among them,
   grazing voraciously.

Devon Church-Goers

[To Susan]

You go in while I walk the grounds.
By the outer wall I find a bubble-up spring.

It's a natural, blue flying buttress....
With a hand-sculpted basin and sidesteps
fashioned by the church masons,
    it, too, is a sacred place.
Pure contents arch off to a valley stream
   where stacked stone banks
      discipline spring flow
  spiriting zealously to The Channel.

Standing under the sky,
  in earshot of your fine high voice
swelling a communion rite inside
    I enjoy this link-up.
Here is a coupling of stream and church
      into one architecture
  wherein a prayer-house genuflects
    to lovely gleaming nature.

Or vice-versa? Does it matter what's
    upstream or down,
   what's source-spring or river?

In there, you resuscitate with
 ultimate bread and wine.
 Out here, I drink first flavour,
and lick my soul into its original shape,
 like a stray mud-mussed feather.

Fragment

Above sleep's dim wetlands,
along the red-tipped rimrocks of rude awakening,
I am an edgy, darting dragonfly.
I peer through the skylights
of my vast odd wings.

Sea Change

Behind forty bent backs I sit
watching for cheat-sheets and other old tricks.
My students are at the oars.
Beneath them unfurls a blue squiggly sea....
One stretches,
puffs up his cheeks
like I did a lost Autumn
in similar straits.

I remember sitting for a test
on poetry — a subject I despised above all!
I jerked bolt upright, sighed loudly and sinkingly
(for the benefit of the teacher and my classmates)
and whispered:
"I'd rather do anything than this: even write the stuff!"
Now, in this gusty rain-swept November,
my toiling class a small scattered fleet ahead of me,
I do just that.

Among Young Bohemians

Hey, there's old Rimbaud again —
    come back as a
rock-screamer on Montreal's Main.
He's slouched over a beer with a nouveau James Dean....
Stars of a sullen
            chic video
they buff their artful acts
            while downtable,
    in darkly gleaming biker regalia,
a Westmount Gertrude Stein
        bullyrags an Alice B.

Say F., aging bohemian
    and drinking buddy,
we've caught the latest parade.
The young flash
        their latest don't-remove-the-label dreams.
See those filmy eyes,
        the stark apocalyptic poses,
fresh mouths pursed around
        the small change of cynicism.

They're so precious, F.
Young pretence wears a marvellous, sheer dress.
Yesterday-born,
        they are gorgeous,
despite the strain of aping deities
        from La Vie Silente.

They redeem us.

In sympathetic magic they exhibit a faith
        once our own.
These kids copy
      — not Kerouac, Holiday, Pollock, Monroe —
          but us.
The old con-gods of fashion wear thin,
but youth that can't help but reveal its lovely self
      plays this phoney old world again....

Yucatan

{For Sandor]

I'm on literary duty in The Yucatan.
By a hotel's smooth jade pool, I sit
encouraging my stepson to write a journal
for the school-time he's missing.

He just suffered his mother's lecture
how tv back home is switching
his once airy imagination for dry tortilla.
He's sentenced now to a lengthy entry,
cruel and unusual punishment in these days
of human sacrifice to Nintendo.

While a cricket chants lost Toltec participles
from fronds above, I remind him
that all we know of this peninsula's history,
including the drama of blood-smeared obsidian
and slab, comes from writing
(from this self-sacrificing cramp of the hand.)
The pen alone preserves truly
the green scuttle of the iguana,
tail lashing in the idol's cracked maw.
Like writers, these beings persist
among the ruins, nourish the forgetful survivors.

But to him, I guess, the past's mossy glyphs
mean little: he wants mostly to play
on sunny heaps, timelessly.
I'm flooding on in this vein passionately
when I notice that he,
likely thrilled by tales of human gore,
or the superb oddness of iguanas,
has drifted off elsewhere, or right here
scribbling furiously....
Well, he has begun — the high priest's limb
darts and stabs, though without its own agonies yet.
"Ignore the growing pains in the thumb," I advise.
"Starting's easy; the hard part's keeping going."
The Mayas pierced their bodies to appease eternity.
Writers trek the broken world on their hands.

Meniscus:
An Essay on Water Striders

Under tremendous pressure,
    water concedes these striders not drown.
Charmed lives, they ply
    Christ-style on this brook
while I stand,
    staggered by the parables
like rainbow trout erupting
    from some undercut of mind.

If only my boot were of a kind
    faithful enough for this slick void.
If only they were magic lifeboats
    buoyed by the grace of physics:

"Air pressure's downward force stymies
    the upward energy of water
molecules, whose force would otherwise
    extend everywhere equally.
Thus do molecules on the surface of depths
bond more firmly laterally..."

to form a skin vital with weightless flies:
  sci-fi taxi dancers
    hustled by trout
 and the face-down imaginings of poets,
doomed Ophelias,
   dry unfestive Hamlets
interrable in any grace,
     gravity,
 body of fluid, or flesh —

concrete-shoed dreamboats
 clutching at one water-logged trope alone —
that on an imagination clear in its intent
 to shoulder the world's full weight,
they shall stride out free.

Rest-Stop
at a Lake Superior Mill-Town

The mill's black truncheon
      overshadows
  the settlement.
The nearby bay's the weirdest
      wall-eyed green.
At the counter I chide the locals
  by announcing if I lived here
"I'd maybe sell two-headed fishing lures....
And your air, by the way, sure tastes like vinegar!"
Noting my crack, the owner
   oddly yellow and lean
 offers to supply the fries.
I nod, cough,
     and jerk my thumb at the sky.
Of the tower of smoke, he explains:
"We call it the flyswatter. At least it keeps
     the mosquitoes down!"
Chewing grease, I joke,
"This town must walk the scalpel
between black humour and cancer!"
He drops his jaundiced eyes.
    Silence descends,
  a sharp and deadly rain.

Babyface

You're aging, pal.
Your once sweet babyface
is sagging down.
In this ruined landing-mirror,
an oceanbottom map
of crevassed, mould-gold deeps,
your face is that of Columbus
shipped home the hard way,
spun into chains,
dreaming of the last audience with his cold
disposing sovereign.

Oh, this world is a mansion of greed,
blind ruthlessness, court treachery,
and the necessity to enslave
or slaughter the lovely and innocent.
Searched by our own look on the steep stairs
we shudder at our compromise,
for as long as we can afford.
The dawn must bring a new redeeming adventure!
Award me one more chance, Prince,
and I'll resuscitate myself,
set out, cross gulfs, discover once more
and lay waste another Earthly paradise.

— September, 1992.

Citycountry

Climbing back of the cabin
  up the stream's spate,
I am in strong reverie:
  warblers vamp ecstatically —

Crepuscular light
  from the busted storm
stuns me too
  — I am a green apostle,
a wide-eyed eremite
  glittering with rain-globes
off the needles I float through.
  I chant to myself:
    I belong here.

Then the old panic returns:
  I've been enlightened in this locale before
    till I wigged out.
I voiced bush lyrics
  (woven of blue-jay feathers,
    porky quills, weasel bones)
in a velcro and video age
  — trying to unleash a fresh poetic rage
but growing swamp-loco and plain loopy
  — a moon-weeper,
      coyote dueter,
forlorn wanker at country drive-ins,
  crazed by loneliness.

Again the city reared above the bushline of fantasy,
　　in its beautiful
　　　　blue poisoning of twilight,
seductive
　as a remote raptor's screams.

I return to the metropolis
　　mostly willingly....
I strive within high close walls
　　　like an ancient Chinese poet
　reinstated to his rightful place
　　in the great bureaucracy.
I make flying visits to that other country,
　　　hover a moment
　like a street-lamp over a beaver pond,
　　　return again
to linger regretfully downtown,
　　a firefly on a corner.
I'm an outlander in two different
　　sites of dreams.

Here at the trail's top, finally,
　　my mind rests.
Among half-shorn ridges
　　　the lake below blues off,
　　a dog-legged dance floor
　in a smoke-filled Montreal brasserie.
Frogs chime like a truck of beer empties.
My face in this slopeside pool's
　　a small pale cloud
hiking through a glass skyscraper's heart.

Muse
on de Bullion Street

May parades green-gold.
Winter's stays are broken.
Across the road the high old dame
that January grippe failed to kill
reclaims her balcony.

Her gaze re-acquaints itself
with Spring's lovely world....
It takes in all the street's inhabitants,
pets repossessing sudden flowerbeds,
even, over my computer, me
lapped by this window's gilt grime.

It's her annual rite,
this careful inventory
of de Bullion's vital elements,
especially the poets, artists, and loonies
exiting blinking from the lowrents....
She leans over the rail
an ancient marquise in her box
squeezing her brow,
or nodding and clapping loudly.

And how they step out, as if just for her:
the muscleman in green plastic and swimmer's goggles;
in her pink parachute-silk suit,
the Wind-propelled Girl who artfully
conducts from within Fall leaf whirls;
under his threadbare China robe
the poet who inconsolably beds down
in the Mount Royal cemetery
on Anna of Siam's tomb.

When this column of mooncalfs has done its turn,
I too shall perform my latest piece.

Our fresh spring outfits donned,
we earnestly seek her sanction
for our latest claims to original vision.

Monstrous Restoration Fantasy: Storm over Montreal

Big thunder over downtown
        suggests Godzilla
come to sup on slurry
    in the St. Lawrence River.
What an eco-recovery project that'd be!
Quebec
        at last
            proffered a more potable purity....

Of course provincial politicos
        separatist
            federalist
    would suss it another way —
            one more reason
                (indisputable)
to erect a bigger hydro-electric 'James Bay':

"We need juice to zap
        this vast green spoiler —
            It's the only way.
Native land claims? Forget 'em.
    It's a national emergency!"

I envision the North's redemption,
    Japanese grade-B.
I'm dreaming now:
    the two behemoths turn and meet.
The great scaled one,
   jaws full of detergent, wagging condoms,
spots the southing super-pylon's rapacious reach.

The horizon echoes
    with the ire of inflamed amphibian.
Great shuddering howls,
    the whack of sparks encroach.
The premier's desk-lamp won't stop flickering.

Ah, blessed brown-out!
    The world righted....
  So the detritus settles —
Our waters return pollutant-free....

No,
   I've been too optimistic:
the bestial sounds falter,
     disaster has struck!
        Godzilla's toast.
Our millennial salamander's
       quaint history....

"Rest assured,
    loyal Quebecers,
the environmentalists
     (and Cree)
will accept our collective destiny!"

Crestfallen,
   I'm about to order my new world's leader
      back underground,
when real storm gusts rip my balcony perch,
       sobering me.
Up off the table
     my first drafts whirl like little Mothras.
    They're off towards the river....
  Reinforcements! Reinforcements!
     — True-Light cavalry.

Godspeed,
     godspeed,
my diminutive, impossibly brave
     otherworldlings.

Moment
at a Garden Party

Studying antique-store photos with my friends
suddenly I get the joke
that lumps us with our quaint ancestors
beaming out of time.

They, too, were the future
and first in all the astonishing,
                        astonished world.
In the latest model
of Reality's chrome-tipped roadster
they pose exuberantly,
their light-bright eyes and mouths
full of fresh gestures and answers.

Our hopes and theirs rhyme
just like that far cloud
        and its shadow
contracting on a line
of underexposed jagged hills.

These brown snaps capture
us perfectly, shivering
my spine.
I look above them to see
the green-blue rushing horizon.

Knights at
the Chemical Dump

[For David Tabakow]

Nature-lovers stuck in town,
    we make do.
Breathing serrated puffs
  of acid and sulphur
we hike the shore of the big
    ruined river,
inside the city's drab heart.

Contemporary Gawains we are
  aiming still for that old Green
      Chapel. We're lost
  in a latter-day Wilderness
of Wirral, with the Frost fences,
     splinter heaps,
troll ponds brewing heavy metals.

Behind irony's visors,
    we crack wise
over the ooze of hydrocarbon beauties,
    the rapids slain
 by Fast Eddies,
     cromlechs stuffed
with burnt dynamos, a Nature gone
  toxic beyond all hint of Faery.
Redemption's a slain hope, we agree,
     on this sunken flat.

Crestfallen,
    we turn home,
  when coming into an oxbow
we halt, stunned by autumn light.
Smudge pots,
    roach-limbed cranes,
industrial detritus gone all golden
    teasing-fragile, immanent —
they seem impossibly beautiful and perfect!

Then we remember Bertilak,
  the magic Green Knight...
squared off laughing
    with the naive young paladin!
In one stroke,
  Arthur's boy beheaded
    the natural giant,
who just scooped His head back up
    with eyes shining and widening grin.

The Escape Attempt:
An Anti-Semiotic Song

Dancing alone
  in my farmhouse parlour
I glance down
  at my wild body's
intent pattern.

It strikes me then
  (from reading certain fashionable texts)
that these convulsions
      of the flesh
are an arbitrary semiotic
      — an ideological shuffle —
as divorced from "reality"
      as I am now from you.

They are an art
  fidgeting on clear exclusion.
Like a winter fly
  mounting this pane,
they hunger with
    (and to impose)
only their own oppressive,
  dull-winged point of view....

In a glorious
   (maybe reactionary)
        revolt
of individual subjectivity,
        I decide it means piss-all
     — this fly-on-a-wallflower theory.
I torque, flounce
   back to my perfect solipsistic trance
  indifferent that destiny is social destiny.

I sweat off all critical considerations concerning
        intention,
          sign,
        signified,
whether this self-sufficient
   enchanting frenzy
        is bounded,
          booted,
   politically suspect,
or the plaintive, ample, post-postmodernist dance
   of the abandoned,
        visionary heart.

Country Dark

Beyond my cabin walls
the bare, creaking woods....
Only night murmurs now
from crickets freezing in funeral
suits of dew.

The next farm over
the mutt howls at length
then stifles all
but his yipping
at a bad dream
or tumbling star.

I still myself too.

Cold, wild-eyed on this bed
I think
of thinking no more of you.

At the River's Side

This Spring, I'm back.
Alone.

There are the willows'
felted blooms,
unravelling green cresses,
and a cold-slugged trout

— he's one of those who,
last Fall,
swaggered brilliantly around our thighs,
still unhooked.

Reawakened to life's
next passion and amnesia,
he remains a sojourner in the river
of all things hurrying past
except for a startling moment, him,
alone once more
at the first and last.

Evening Walk
by Lake Superior

[for M.N.]

The once familiar point gleams
on the rose edge of light.

Under my sandals, beach cobbles
grind louder, hollowly.

Twenty years ago I worked up here
planting spruce and pine.
Abandoned all summer,
my girl stayed in Toronto.

I wrote her now and then, of course,
and got delicate loving replies.
I reread both sets recently: yes,
I've got copies of my own!
Her letters are adorable and touching.
Mine? I was a cold striver.
They are slick with the impermeable
self-absorption
of the callow up-and-comer.

— Someone who came and went
ranting interminably about 'Number One,'
until inevitably she sent him
on his thunderstruck way.
(Somehow, I'd neglected after graduation
to propose to her.)

She, eventually, married another,
and, in character, I believed I had invented misery.
In true sixties manner, I drank
and smoked excessively.
My heart, you see, was a fire-scar
my ego a logging waste,
my daily route a trophy hall of stuffed hyperboles.

My never-to-be-forgotten first love
has gone off an age (over Superior's wrinkled dim plane),
but haunts me now, a world or two after,
with excruciating sweetness and the exquisite fret
of blue driftglass fingered in half-light.

Time is irretrievable
like the persuasions of old self-love.
I adored myself passionately,
cultivated Power and Regret,
but too few regrets.

My heart's been a spruce-tangle
few have pushed through.
Now, suddenly, before me upon this memory beach,
no longer exiled after all these years,
her love steps into full view
not ghost-like but like a body and soul released
 — so grace-filled, so nakedly beautiful and real,
I mutter awkward words.
Behind my eyes, from a tremendous gulf,
sweep in waves of tears.

Old Fisherman

In that country of sunken rivers
he awoke one morning
to the full sound of a stream.

Nowhere at hand
could he recall abundant water.

But there, in the wrinkled
basin of his palm,
something brightened
like an old desire
or a re-opened wound.

Down his fingers' creases,
past his thumb's heap,
a brook splashed
into a perfect pond.

Something else shone!
A great rainbow trout, small as a minnow,
darted, thrashed, and hung.

After the Flu: Spring

I sit here
and watch the sun
gild the old streets.

Ten days in bed
can clog the mind with low things:
bad debt, sick self and
disheartened friends,
till it feels like a St. Henri alley
full of three-legged chairs, wall-eyed tv's
sway-backed mattresses,
a veritable dump
of *vis inertia*
— unsprung, frost-seized, irredeemable.

Then comes the sun
grinning, munificent.
Her prodigal red fingers
are never spent.

Woman Bathing
in the Rouge River

[To Susan]

You breast-stroke in the crimson,
cedar-edged pool.

Your hair is a snood
   of backwards silver,
your face, an oval of purest joy,
   while your body is
      a goldenness
streaming through prismatic water....

What you inhabit grows
      marvellous,
   and becomes you.

This poem embraces you
      as does its poet,
a well of customary reserve,
   in a root-watering displacement.
Love's liquid eye is possessed
   and spilled by a gorgeous mote.

Join me
   and let me become you
      — as you become me.
Let my heart's full vessels
         tide up
            and float.

Reflections of the Lake Superior Shoreline

In the darkening waters at my feet
    the star-topped cliffs —
(crystal grommeted curtains
      rising up
  at the sky behind me) —
lie in perfect imitation.

They reappear
  both high and deep.
As I wade in
     step-by-step
  on invisible slick cobbles —
a star-cast shadow precariously
     climbing an image —
there's no mistaking this fear of falling.

Fall where? — Not down,
  but into these imaged stone walls,
     a disaster met
  at right angles to the axis of intent?

Failing to scale vision,
  shall I be pressed in stone
where, with fish fossils,
  they will find my bones,
and flattened question marks of eyes?

The water's cold
  and getting deep.
Nocturnal gill beings nibble.
    This stretch —
where big lake and unspoiled country meet —
  foams along its coast
    with savage allusiveness.

I should have turned in early
    beneath my tent,
having ankle-waded the damp beach....

But the trouble-maker in me couldn't sleep.
  It left me in here,
      up to my neck,
  at the cliff reflection's sharp brink.
  I can now almost reach silvery fish
          breaking the surface,
clouding through spaces between stars.

Winter Lovers

Over the city a last
autumn sky....
Jets scrape to the bone.
Down Sherbrooke Street the pale sun
goes out in a kindling of shadows.
Late birds blink
above sacking-wrapped tree trunks,
too late now to set out
down that cold violent coast.
Winterers, we huddle
and adore the narrow eye of fire.
We weigh rumours of enchanting
golden city-states in the far south.
Maybe this New Year's we'll take a look.
Meanwhile, love,
let's tangle our bodies and dream
we are jaguars playing on a hot white beach.

The Old Indians

Their physical bravery is
what amazes me: their marvellous wild incursions.
It was individual, perfect, and gunshot proof
(unlike their lithe, too-human, tragic bodies.)
Courage was a shiny talon
protruding from a way of life
overseen by eagles.

Our way was part of a buzzard's purview!
Or a snake in a sunken culvert den.
And as far as our courage was and is,
who knows?
If what I see here goes,
then it's just the farm-boy's swagger
or the strut and hipshot pose of drugstore cowboys
in a sun-slugged Wyoming town
where nursery turf shrivels on grit
and shrinks from the lines of bronze plains' grass
pluming from cracks in the road.

Drinking Beer on a
Sand-Hill in Northwestern Nebraska

The bison have long gone
west of the West
straggling up in gold-flecked lines
onto the smokey plateau of dreams.

Only their trails remain, scored
into the bluffsides and cottonwood coulees,
maintained by a few mule deer
and a slaughterhouse alumni
of steers.

The white man's vision proved
too powerful by far and near.
Into the unconscious
we coralled the old frontier.
The Garden's trampled for good.

Progress drives one way, it seems:
to red metal,
bone, alkali,
and strained imaginings....

No resurrection-song can unearth the time for long.
Wovoka, Buffalo Bill, Rough Riding Teddy
— all the tall misty-eyed horsemen —
staged one comeback too many,
ate dirt, curled their toes up, went dumb.

Still, a hundred paces from where I sit,
churning the White River drybed
red pickups shoot local stetsons into town.
They are hunting rosé, beefsteak, and jukesong
sung by 'cowboys' born too late for the West.

Each Friday, in downtown Summit, Nebraska,
their ghost-dance transforms a drab hall.
Square-jawed Dukes and frilly Annies
stomp, whoop, and holler
in gaudy western boots and duds.

Smile grimly under your hill
sad prophet of return, Wovoka!
Here on a bluff, don't I talk high and mighty?
Who doesn't cry after spirits
and floor-pounding sets? Shush!
There's something on the old river trail
 — hooves sorting the moonlit dust.

( )

Going through the Poetry Files

Not many poems here!
I finger the pinched file marked, "Happily in love...."

The next, slumping under its own weight,
is inscribed, "Love Lost: Collected Laments."

I was I suppose too spellbound
riding the neap tides of flushed erotic nights
to dismount and write.

I preferred red roses blowing in my hair,
wild, mauve irises below,
and throaty ululations.

Thus few works in the Love file —

a few transcribed cries, primal
and stark as pictographs
anticking on Lake Superior rocks.

I'm less graphic now, just literate and lorn.
I have no problem writing at all —
dropping a tear in the Historic Site's turnstyle
I take the full blue tour.   (}

My verse is just elegy.
Like a shore-swell
my hand motions on and on,
cresting far below the gorgeous red dancers.

West Coast Pier

At China's end of the pier
are sunlight, clouds, wide windiness
and the blue, imperial surge of the sea.

Here
like a Toronto runaway from The Sixties,
my country fetches against a final rail
and runs out of itself.

On this long holiday weekend
I sit and watch the citizenry
mostly white and well-tailored
out from the sad clean suburbs
pursuing some barely recalled
reflex of westering.

Alone or in pairs, gazes flat,
they come to a halt, a little desperate
as if nothing could be as disheartening
as what they've laid eyes on here.

It's revolting!:
the pricey fish snacks, the tourist mob, the din
of neighbours' kids' spoiled roughhousing
— the huge families of immigrant Asians
crab-fishing in lively lines
eastwards down the pier.

My Antique
Coin Collection

Finally I'm getting rid of it,
flogging it to its brassy heir:
up-to-date hard currency.

True, I have only to hold onto these golden eggs
laid by Luna Moth Time
and, in my lifetime,
they'd keep me.

But decades have spent themselves
since these caesars enthralled me.
They have presided here unredeemed
and coldly immutable.
Under their imperium
my world's sagged.

I am the pocket-hole they've worn,
the piece their thumbs rubbed thin.

Surprises

Sometimes
the time is so long between

like an old mountain
a man forgets all.

He is surprised by an offer
but also more — that the terrain of
self, itself is found
changed,

a presumed green and
lushness lost,

the familiar forest scraped,
the heart reduced
to the moon's chilled pond.

It's the same with you I'm sure

which makes for one more shock

the dealing of
parts of our selves
back and forth here
in this dark Algoma motel

pieces which glitter in the palm
as ruby-grained and beautiful
as petrified wood.

Departures

There is a country I visit
  under starshine now
or in blue moonlight's
    terra incognita.

For me
    this is a departure.
I was a compiler of
    daylight fact:
my brain wasn't quiet
  till I had secured every ravine,
conquered every hill,
  and logged the correct term
      for each flower....

By head-rote I acquired
  what I should have gained
        by heart
  and thereby learned —
the sites and names of everything
  trespass against enchantment.

Despite such insight
  what's left recovers slowly.
Like a rare nocturnal animal
  it shies at the shadow.

Night discovers me again.
  in this sidereal meadow.
The land tilts to a spruce swamp,
    dreaming fog.
   Coyotes hunt here....

To my left, one croons
  and my mind lunges that way.
I recall the tale of a farmer
  waking one night
to the bangs of his husky
   gone off its chain.

The following Spring,
  its lunar eyes flashed
blue dozens from the bushline.

Retro-Man

I wrestle with the car-radio.

An old hit surfaces
   then sinks insidiously.

Here's another — same message:
   I did my best, pretty darlin',
from now on I'll do better!

More water.
   My heart, that memorable loser,
lip-synchs its unique mass history.

Roses are red, my love, violets are blue.

My first fiancée tossed my ring
   into a Toronto dumpster.

Baby, baby, where did our love go?

Riding the train
   out to set up a West Coast love-nest,
we turned off and uncoupled
   in bitter, flat Alberta.

Ode to a
Country Stone Pile

Here is an altar of the world's bones.
This red sun-up along the scrubby
pasture's edge,
it mounds and elbow-curves
at length and with grace,
like a giant's cast-off limb
or the shape of the limit of throwing
by dead-tired men on tractors and carts
at long furrow's end.

From fractured glacial-scatter
they have fashioned the white arm
of the Great Being
— like paleontologists
who rebuild thunder-lizards
(remodelled obscurely on themselves...)
from a single chalky femur.

Six layers of simple Sawyerville farmers
had other things on their minds
as they cast about!
Intent on their plough's stoney road
they sculpted their worship mound
sidelong and perfectly unknowing.

[Untitled]

i

On this wild
   northern beach,
jobfree at last,
   I stretch my sky-hued tent
         fishbelly tight
   and make off feeling poetic.

I'm intent on finally doing
   nothing in particular,
here where there are only
   marvellous particulars,
on this lake-isle
   splayed like a vast Lot
         mineralized
for ignoring the divine injunction:
      not to look back
upon God's erasure and cleansing
   in the form
         (this time)
   of a Wisconsinian ice-sheet....

Circling this place,
   I respond to mink tracks
delicately incising spits;
   wind-aria through white pike-grins;
         clay text
of indecipherable water-sculpted script;

and a bright red shore-creeper
edging speculatively out
    then slithering back
        like the "Z" in zen,
over a scraped white void of beach....

ii

I've despoiled
    this most perfect world
        and myself again —
fleeing from my constructions
        just to repeat them.
I circled an island
    as an untasked being
then retraced my tracks
        in mind and fact
in order to contrive a poem.

Falling,
    I tighten and tie
the world to my pole and pegs.
    One blue heaven
            thrumbs
while another sags, so a man
    left to his restless self and vexed,
can wall and roof his own bright freedom.

Ascent

We are making love — she above,
  me wingless beneath
when suddenly I realize
  her mind's elsewhere.

Beware the musician lover who
    professionally
  accompanies ceremonies.
Head tossed, spine
  arched like a Celtic harp,
    she's rehearsing.

On my chest
  her hands practise scales.
Her pursed lips
   delicately hum.
  She lifts me into air.

Rimer's Lament

With what ingratitude
the great poems
supersede their makers!

For eons, maybe eternity,
these second-hand immortals sashay
up the marble halls
of the fancy anthologies.
All eyes dilate on them alone.

How they strut,
how quickly forget
from whose sparse, difficult lives
they sprang.

At Oblivion's hostel
they dump the delicate, spent tongues
that made them.

Psycho-Gothic

He was raised in the dreary ruin:
adult hopes.
Though publically educated
he attended the exclusive finishing school
of petit bourgeois disillusion.
His parents bore no smarter,
more painstaking son,
or one by his own monumental exertions
more likely to supersede and betray them.
They expelled him from the family manse,
Vain Aspirations.
He throve of course,
despite a tic of sinister negativity
that threatened to puncture every triumph,
yet deep down he enjoyed, in success,
an even greater nullity.
Each morning from a haunted,
fretful sleep he rose,
a monster of intense ambition.
He shovelled away mountains daily
— mostly from the *massif* within.
Few strangers meeting him could resist
(or long endure)
the beauty and monotony
of his odes to personal disenchantment.
Tutored by his parents' pessimism,
he was a grand failure,
doomed forever to desperate success,
unlike them.

Morning After:
At the Dacha

At breakfast, reading great Russian writers
before trying my own hand,
I find them likewise inconsolable.
When love's thwarted, worse, lost,
they make a lovely mournful sound
— Chekhov, Brodsky, Akhmatova, Akhmadulina....

My heart cries and the hill-poplars
fling their blighted gold.
Fall's first frost flashes and fades,
— save in my love's departing steps
glittering angrily over the lawn.

My pen clumsies after.... Here in Canada
I am twice bereft — of her
and alluring words like theirs.
At my plain maple desk I mumble like a character
from century-old Russian literature,
— a tongue-tied, wall-eyed mujik
whose thick memorials
chafe and itch, coarsest homespun.

I scratch doggedly,
deep bush-work,
hoping an unforgettable native cry
will make, if not her,
foreign poets sigh.

Doll's House

A doll, I endure.

Seized crystals, my eyes
train on the hallway
where my Mistress
ripples satins and furs,
effortlessly comes and goes...

— a giantess who looks like me!

I wonder about this constantly:
how she is now everywhere
now nowhere.
I can't budge.

In nearby stone bowls
the rooted plants
twine towards the sun.
Its alluring light only
crazes my yellowing porcelain.

Did some forced union
between troll and human
produce unequal twins:
one shrunken and paralytic
who needs help to cry or stare?

You've not heard this tale
— a beauty and her stunted sister....
There enters a handsome prince.
All are secretly appalled
(though claim it just)
as he shuns the shiny belle
to kiss the enduring loveliness
behind my massive look.

It's a fable I invented
— unable even to wince
after the real boy rushed on by
slinging his roses on my lap!

Later,
nude in the shining air
they giggle and pause —
when suddenly reddening,
one twists my gaze elsewhere.

Poetry

It visits mostly
when I go tramping
fields and woods.
It arrives as on a scented spring dawn
when after working late,
I paced the bushline
and heard the lovely sharp wranglings of fox pups
rough-housing in first territories;
or the time on a red evening,
after a day's drudgery
I crept quietly into tall rushes.
I had become transfixed repeatedly with how,
after my final intruding step
the stark fresh shout of peepers
snapped off perfectly
like green volcanic glass.
Their fresh chant gathered me in,
then poised me.
So poetry comes and goes with me, despite
I'm beside myself with worries.
There exists this world of fine, pure solitude,
perfect intimacy with strangeness
and seizing sounds and soundlessness....
Was this not how it was when the gods
visited men?
Now there are no gods —
just sheer wild intercessions
along a spruce-line, down a stream-crossed trail.

Autumn Dress Code

On exquisite edge, leaves model
red hues of goodbye.
One behind the other, each parades off
over the ranges
of ravishing departure.

Spruce-bogs
glow
with the Galloise cellophane
of last flies.

Sleek skunks
nightclub to the headlight electric,
sashay under helpless hurtling
pickups.

Having slaughtered my way to my cabin
I'm spooked before sleep
by the flamboyant submission of their bones.

I'd forgot how
frost embalms grassblades,
silvers twigs, makes
fine grave-goods of seed-crowns.

I'm a survivor at the funeral.
I'm a wallflower among
fey dancing dandies.
I couldn't feel more out of it
in this will to live —
a cheap hand-me-down suit.

Gothic Piscatorial

The stars emerge
over the private brook.
Big bow-backed trout
slip from the shadow of stones
to gather in the lit pool.
They spread like a black laquer fan
across dim currents
that tickle and ease them
like the hand of a lordly angler
stirred by hungry dreams.
Here in a beleaguered band,
they pass the night
feeding fussily
but with vicissitude's sharp appetite,
and brooding behind scarred lips
upon a lifetime of caution:
the ferocious self-discipline
which brilliantly preserves
their straitened, gallant portion.
Few beings know such lonesomeness,
yet in this blue pool
a pure camaraderie coheres
among those who've endured
on the estate of some predatory knight
now sleeping off his trout-flesh with one care....

Gorgeous generations darted here
until the final deadly jerk.
In the brief interval, in subsided fear
they rise to pale starlight
settling like a ghost mayfly hatch.
Like monks at a midnight communion
they feast on silvery nothings here.

Four A.M. Piece

From where
   are we talking about?

From the night's edge.

Let the half-light
    do the talking....
Listen to your
   dawn-mutterings, when
     the eye-sockets of language
      are shadows.

Here is your limberlost
   canoe-camp talk,
where the snipped, watch-spring stars
    hang out,
and from opposite sides of the lake
   an owl and a loon
    make gothic chit-chat....

What poetry loves is solitude,
   the wake of conscious prostration
     or disaster.
    It likes to trek and dabble
     in The Burn,
the lithe, deep-bottom voice,
    the dark fish rising
   lonely at sundown
    (or dawn)
at the mouth of a Lovelorn River.

Not just talk —
        utterance.

To write like this,
    get struck
  the only way that matters...
out of nowhere,
  out of a blind spot.
      Have the light
  at the tunnel's end turn
into the proverbial storm-lamp
    wielding another train.
  Suffer an earthquake
    on your wedding day.

The only consolation is the language
      that'll catch you up,
string a taut wire through your gape,
  and drag you down
    to writhe and splutter
        in its wake.

It's the lingo that
  nightsides you,
    turns you black,
     wide-bodied,
with a pickerel's moony eyes —
  the better to observe how,
    under your shallow boat,
      gorgeous shadows
    have clustered all along.

NOTES ——————————————————————————————